I Spy
coloring book
for Kids

This Book belongs to:

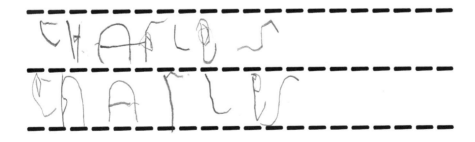
CHARLES
CHARLES

I SPY WITH MY LITTLE EYE
SOMETHING STARTING WITH

It's an Acorn

I SPY WITH MY LITTLE EYE
SOMETHING STARTING WITH

It's
Bread

I SPY WITH MY LITTLE EYE
SOMETHING STARTING WITH

It's
Candles

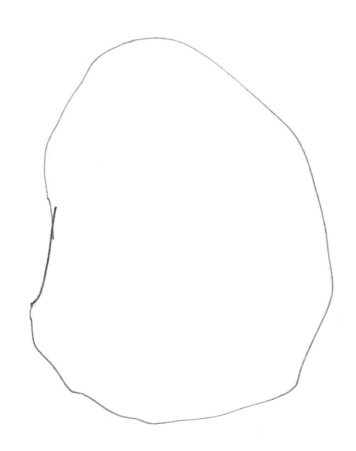

I SPY WITH MY LITTLE EYE
SOMETHING STARTING WITH

It's
Dessert

I SPY WITH MY LITTLE EYE
SOMETHING STARTING WITH

It's
Eating

I SPY WITH MY LITTLE EYE
SOMETHING STARTING WITH

It's a Fig

I SPY WITH MY LITTLE EYE
SOMETHING STARTING WITH

It's Gravy

I SPY WITH MY LITTLE EYE
SOMETHING STARTING WITH

It's
Ham

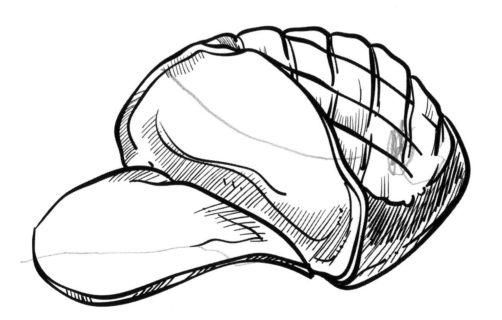

I SPY WITH MY LITTLE EYE
SOMETHING STARTING WITH

It's an Indian

I SPY WITH MY LITTLE EYE
SOMETHING STARTING WITH

It's
Jam

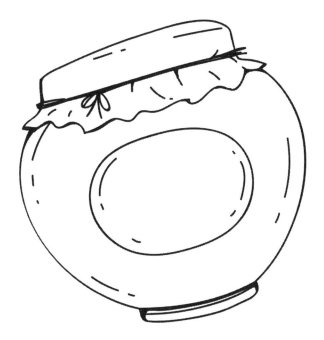

I SPY WITH MY LITTLE EYE
SOMETHING STARTING WITH

It's Kitchen

I SPY WITH MY LITTLE EYE
SOMETHING STARTING WITH

It's a Leaf

I SPY WITH MY LITTLE EYE SOMETHING STARTING WITH

It's
Meat

I SPY WITH MY LITTLE EYE
SOMETHING STARTING WITH

It's a Napkin

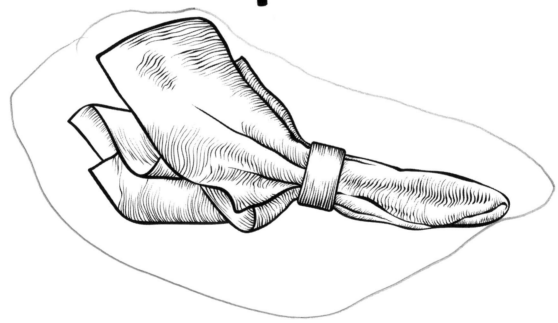

I SPY WITH MY LITTLE EYE SOMETHING STARTING WITH

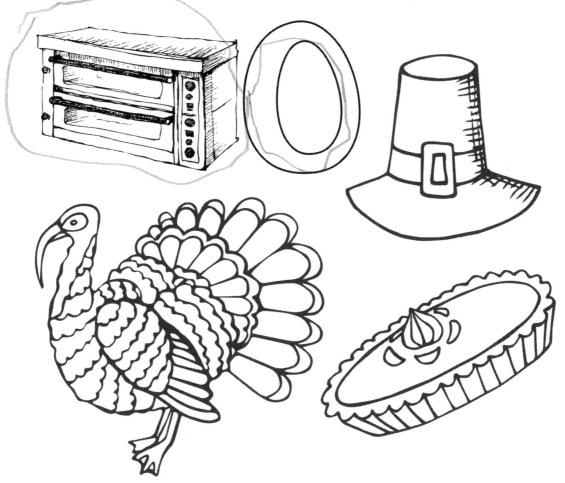

It's an Oven

I SPY WITH MY LITTLE EYE
SOMETHING STARTING WITH

It's a Pilgrim

I SPY WITH MY LITTLE EYE SOMETHING STARTING WITH

It's a Quaint

I SPY WITH MY LITTLE EYE
SOMETHING STARTING WITH

It's a
Roast Turkey

I SPY WITH MY LITTLE EYE
SOMETHING STARTING WITH

It's a Squash

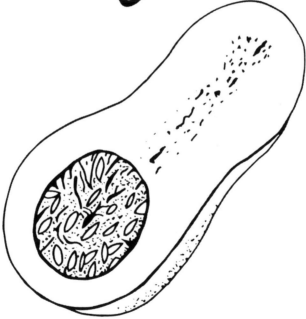

I SPY WITH MY LITTLE EYE
SOMETHING STARTING WITH

It's a Turkey

I SPY WITH MY LITTLE EYE
SOMETHING STARTING WITH

It's
Utensils

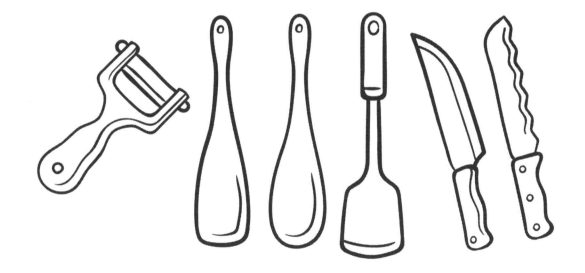

I SPY WITH MY LITTLE EYE
SOMETHING STARTING WITH

It's
Vegetables

I SPY WITH MY LITTLE EYE
SOMETHING STARTING WITH

It's
Wishbone

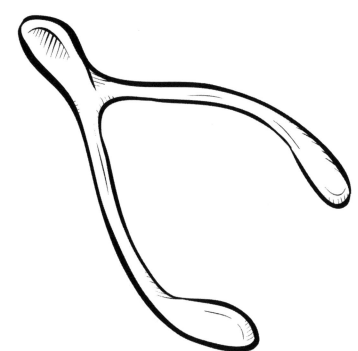

I SPY WITH MY LITTLE EYE
SOMETHING STARTING WITH

It's a Xylophone

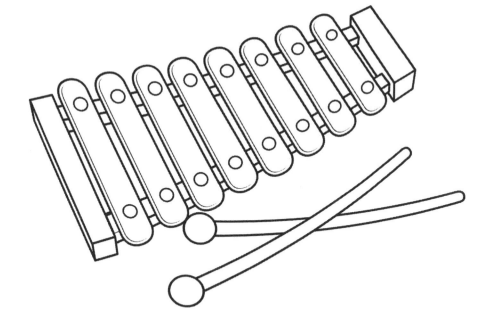

I SPY WITH MY LITTLE EYE SOMETHING STARTING WITH

It's Yams

I SPY WITH MY LITTLE EYE
SOMETHING STARTING WITH

It's
Zucchini

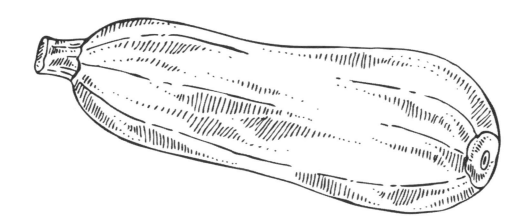

Made in the USA
Las Vegas, NV
04 November 2021